SHORT WALKS AROUND
DARTMOOR

Edited by Aune Harbourne

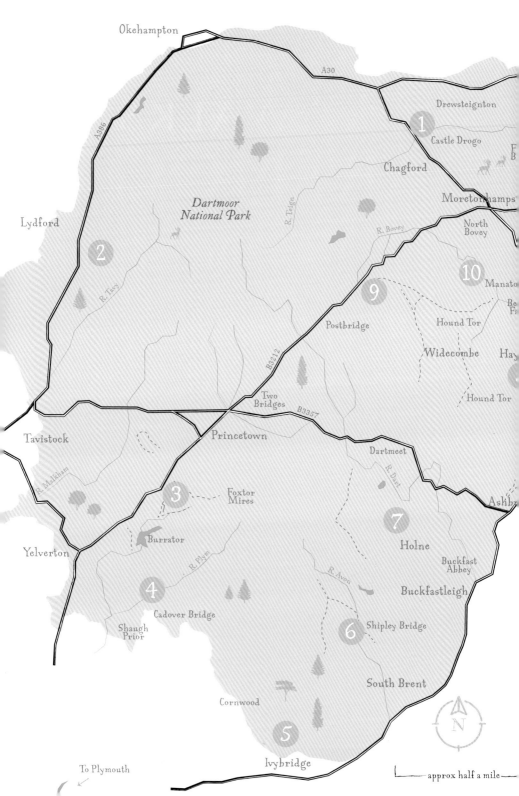

CONTENTS

① WALK 1 Castle Drogo & the Teign Valley | 4.5 miles   7

② WALK 2 Tavy Cleave Valley | 4.5 miles   10

③ WALK 3 Burrator Reservoir & Crazywell Pool | 4.5 miles   15

④ WALK 4 Cadover Bridge & Dartmoor-on-Sea | 4 miles   18

⑤ WALK 5 Harford & Dartmoor Landscape | 3 miles   23

⑥ WALK 6 Shipley Bridge & the Avon Dam | 5 miles   26

⑦ WALK 7 Holne Moor & Wheal Emma | 3 miles   31

⑧ WALK 8 Haytor & the Best Tors on Dartmoor | 6 miles   34

⑨ WALK 9 Yelverton - Warren House & the Land of Mines | 4 miles   41

⑩ WALK 10 Manaton & Manaton Rocks | 3 miles   44

INTRODUCTION

Highland Cow on Dartmoor

Dartmoor has approximately one square mile for each day of the year – 368 to be exact! This sounds like a vast expanse with plenty to choose from for a short walk. However, some of these square miles are on private land, others are under great coniferous forests, and many are extensive tracts of mires. This book of walks will help you find those square miles where you can wander to your heart's content, safe in the knowledge that you will eventually return to your vehicle, and not get lost in this lovely landscape.

Short Walks on Dartmoor is designed to offer you a variety of walks and, providing you encounter reasonable weather conditions, should take you through spectacular countryside. The walks mostly follow tracks and aim to avoid road walking. The sketch maps with each walk are designed to provide you with a rough guide, but it is highly recommended that you invest in a copy of the Ordnance Survey Explorer Leisure Map, number 28, which gives detail at a scale of 1:25,000. It is an extremely large map and is better folded to the portion you need, as many a copy has been whisked away by a spirited Dartmoor gale!

Walking on Dartmoor is one of life's great pleasure although 'forewarned is forearmed' and if you are fully prepared for all eventualities, you will probably sail around the routes wondering what all the fuss was about! There are some wonderful walks waiting for you and we are sure you will enjoy every one of them!

SAFETY FIRST!

Dartmoor is one of the UK's most beautiful places to visit. However, it needs to be treated with respect and walks should recognise that the weather can change in minutes. At the time of printing, the route instructions had been recently walked. Alas as time passes things change, and of course some walkers may interpret details in a different way to that intended; good planning is therefore key! Read the walks through before you start out, compare the sketch map route with your more detailed map and note, in advance, the sort of conditions you are likely to encounter.

Remember to keep an eye on the weather and be prepared to dress for the conditions. Do not walk in sandals or flip flops; walking on Dartmoor, however easy the route, always requires strong, sensible footwear, a good waterproof, an extra layer, sun cream, a hat and a map. A compass or GPS may be useful. As you may be out for a few hours, take something to eat and plenty to drink just in case your energy drains and needs to be recharged. Make sure your mobile phone is fully charged. If possible, let someone know the route you are taking, and your expected return time.

The Ministry of Defence uses a vast area of the northern moor for firing practice and other exercises. Warnings signals from the military include: red flags by day and red lamps by night, indicating that live firing is taking place within the range boundaries, which are themselves marked by red and white poles. When warning signals are displayed do not cross the range boundary. It is always advisable to check details which may be found at:
www.gov.uk/government/publications/dartmoor-firing-programme
@MOD_DIO #moddartmoor

Do not touch any military debris, it may be dangerous. Note the location and inform Police immediately.

Finally, always follow the Countryside Code:
RESPECT – other people by parking carefully and considerately, using car parks where possible (even if this means extending your walk slightly) avoiding driveways and gateways. Leave everything as you find it and give way to other walkers. Always follow the path and avoid off-track areas.

PROTECT – take everything on and off Dartmoor with you, leaving no evidence of your visit. Keep dogs under control, using a lead when other people, dogs and livestock are around, and pick up and take home your dog's poo. Never light a fire or BBQ.

ENJOY – follow signs and local advice, even if it differs from your walking guide. Plan ahead, check the weather and local facilities and walk prepared for every type of climate.

All of this should ensure you have a fantastic day out and return again and again!

Teign Valley

WALK 1

CASTLE DROGO & THE TEIGN VALLEY

Drewsteignton is a small hilltop village on the edge of the Dartmoor National Park. Although the surrounding scenery is not open moorland country, its beauty still proves popular with walkers. Park your car in the square amongst the many granite-built cottages and attractive Holy Trinity Church. Here is the starting place for a circular walk of about four to five miles.

— DISTANCE: 4.5 miles

ⓟ PARKING: Square by Holy Trinity Church
EX6 6QN

Although there are a few short, sharp ascents to come, you start by leaving the square on the road towards Chagford. A little way along, opposite the former village school, there is an obvious track leading off to the left.

This is a section of the famous 'Two Moors Way' route which spans both Dartmoor and Exmoor, plus the many miles of farmland in between. The walks start gently with the path carrying you downwards into the valley of the small tributary stream that runs down to Fingle Bridge. Beyond the stream is a steepish climb passing through Rectory Wood, a reminder that the church once owned great areas of land – called Glebe lands. The hill begins to level out and a gentle drop brings you out to the much-walked Hunters' Path, high above the valley of the Teign. To your left/east is Drewston Common, whilst to your right/west is Piddledown Common.

On reaching a T-junction of paths, you should head west, or right, and soon you will reach a most impressive rocky outcrop, known as Sharp Tor. It is not a typical Dartmoor tor in that it juts out spectacularly from the side of the gorge. It is a good vantage point over the wooded valley way below. Castle Drogo is away to your right and, in the distance, you may be able to pick out the higher northern moors of Dartmoor, Hangingstone Hill, Kestor Rock and Fernworthy Forest. These are just some of the landmarks you may identify whilst taking a well-earned breather.

The track is easy to follow as it contours the hillside. This part of the moor appears in almost every walking book and as a consequence the track, which was only a footstep wide some thirty years ago, is now quite broad. Still, it offers an opportunity to say 'hello' to walkers heading in the opposite direction, so be prepared to be sociable as you head on below Castle Drogo to reach a low spur where the path veers sharply away from the main valley.

You now have a choice, depending on how steep you like your terrain. You may either opt for the short, sharp, steep, short cut down to the bottom of the hill (care and good footwear are needed for this route) or you may prefer the slightly longer but no less beautiful route which follows the track to the right and north for about 400 yards before almost doubling back on itself to reach the same point at Coombe. Head down the road, and after a while keep left heading towards the river, which is wider and more distinct than the stream flowing into it.

The path you now follow is on the left and is known as the Fishermen's Path, which meanders along a fine fishing route. The land is owned by the National Trust who have improved the access and paths over recent years. There are a few minor climbs on the first section, but soon the path becomes a gentle walk with the two miles to Fingle Bridge providing ample time to build up an appetite. In high summer, the woods will seem like a dense verdant jungle, whereas in autumn it is a golden paradise; the changing seasons could not be more obvious.

Fingle Bridge straddles the river at a point where a tributary stream, which rises near Whiddon Down on the A30, enters into this beauty spot. The stream has cut a gap between Prestonbury Castle – an Iron-age Hill Fort – and Drewston Common. The road builders have taken advantage of this deep cleft in the hills to forge a route to Fingle. On fine days it is a very popular spot.

Formerly the Angler's Rest, the Fingle Bridge Inn grew from the humble beginnings of a tea shelter, at the turn of the 19th/20th century, into the fine building you see today. Should you need light refreshment, or a full-blown meal, here would be a good choice. A few hours will probably have elapsed since you set out so, to complete this stroll, follow the road out of Fingle towards Drewsteignton and, after about 500 yards, turn first left onto the path which will take you along the northern limit of Rectory Wood. In about half a mile you will recognise where you were earlier in the day. Follow the track, up and right, back to Drewsteignton.

Although deer are extremely rare on the open moorlands of Dartmoor, they are common in the woods along the Teign Gorge. How quiet and how close you are to the extremes of the day – early morning/ late evening – will govern your chances of spotting them. As you will have spent much of the walk espying Castle Drogo, it may be an idea to incorporate a visit in your day out. The sheltered nature of the Teign Valley makes this a perfect walk on a wet and windy day.

© Pedro Lastra

Fingle Bridge © Simon Nicholson

WALK 2

TAVY CLEAVE VALLEY

There is a large car park beside the A386 road between Mary Tavy and Sourton (EX20 4AL). From the Okehampton direction it is just beyond the cattle grid on your left, where the road enters the open moorland at Willsworthy Down. The reverse applies if you are travelling northwards. The car park is not the nearest point to the area you explore in this outing, but access along the surfaced road towards the Tavy Cleave is restricted to army vehicles visiting Willsworthy. Remember to check that the army are not firing, further information can be found at www.gov.uk/government/publications/dartmoor-firing-programme

---

— DISTANCE: 4.5 miles
(with extension: 6 miles)
ⓟ PARKING: EX20 4AL

This will eventually become a spectacular walk of about four and a half miles, despite starting in decidedly dull surroundings. Taking an uphill, easterly direction, follow the road towards the rifle ranges: it is softer on the feet if you walk beside it. There is a cluster of military buildings at the top of the hill; follow the road as it bends sharply around them. Stay with or beside this road for a further 200 yards. On your right-hand side is a rough track, which goes off at a right-angle. It has a low mound beside it, which disappears very quickly. Follow this track and in a short distance you will reach a fenced-off rifle range with a gate bearing a large letter 'B'. Skirt the right-hand side of the fence and soon you will see a wooden footbridge ahead of you. This is ideal for right-handed walkers who are outward bound and perfect for left-handed walkers who are homeward bound! Precise route descriptions every few yards are no longer necessary once you have crossed the bridge and turned left to follow the leat.

The Reddaford or Mine leat provides an easy way of reaching the Tavy Cleave; after it turns sharply, good views of the country in and around the Tavy Valley will be seen. The small farm on your right is Nattor Farm; as the leat turns to enter the Cleave it passes around the spur which contains Nat Tor itself. Most people fail to notice it as they are distracted by the splendid sight that confronts them, as they peer up through this spectacular rocky canyon.

Eventually the leat ends at a small intake building: a good spot to take a break beneath the great mass of Ger Tor. The going to this point has been decidedly easy but now a bit more care is needed

Tavy Cleave Valley

Tavy Cleave © Mike Frost

as the terra firma is not so firm as you head towards the most striking part of the Tavy Cleave. It is extremely soft in places, mainly so beside the river, as you head eastwards towards a sharp bend.

When the corner is turned, a wonderful sight presents itself – a scene which has been heralded by so many great writers as one of the loveliest on the moor. The Tavy drops steeply through this gorge in a succession of miniature rapids and waterfalls, whilst steep hills rise up on either side, like the walls of a great strong castle. A waterfall is soon encountered. It is a splendid place, and on days when a fierce north-westerly breeze blasts the high northern moors, this deep, steep valley offers shelter.

At this point, various alternatives are open to you; the walk can easily be extended to go as far as the confluence with the Rattlebrook, then head over Hare Tor, before veering south-westwards back to Willsworthy (a total of about six and a quarter miles); or, if you are agile and like a challenge, the north side of the Tavy Cleave, rising straight up from the waterfall, can be climbed. This is a mixture of clitter (rocky debris strewn on the hillside) and vegetation. This should be taken slowly and is not suitable for very young children. On reaching the summit, the most direct way back is over the shoulder of Ger Tor. On a clear day, the Mine Leat will be seen from here and can be reached easily at the point where it sharply turns the corner over the Willsworthy Brook.

Families with young children may wish to retrace their steps because, once the leat is picked up, there are no major ups or downs and a reasonable pace can be maintained back to Willsworthy. This is more of an out-and-back route than many of the other more circular ones, but a visit to this impressive rocky valley should be part of any walker's itinerary.

Tavy Cleave

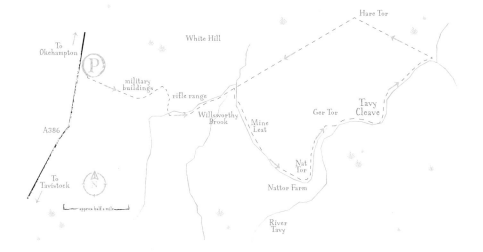

Tavy Cleave

13

Burrator Reservoir

WALK 3

BURRATOR RESERVOIR & CRAZYWELL POOL

This splendid little walk through woods, across open moors and past all manner of interesting objects and historical landmarks, is about four and a half miles. The starting point is a picturesque spot – the diminutive Nosworthy Bridge (PL20 6PF), which straddles the River Meavy, or Mewy, on the north-eastern corner of Burrator Reservoir. There is usually plenty of parking in the car park and vicinity, even if you choose a rare, busy day.

> — DISTANCE: 4.5 miles
> ℗ PARKING: Nosworthy Bridge car park
> PL20 6PF

Head out of the car park towards the Nosworthy Bridge where beside the bridge is a well-defined track that climbs gently north-eastwards. It is your corridor to the moor and should be followed. Almost immediately, a tempting wooded path leads away to the left, but do not be distracted as your route ascends to the moor to a more open and less peopled environment.

The track is stony and climbs steadily but if you can persuade yourself (and followers) that the effort is worth it, then your rewards will come later and will be considerable. The remains of farm buildings will be seen below you on your right; all the people who farmed in the feeder valleys to Burrator had to leave the watershed for pastures new, although some were allowed to stay on until they passed away.

By keeping the forest on your left, you will eventually reach a gateway onto the open moor. The track is less demanding on the feet and only needs to be followed for a few hundred yards. As you curve around the first hill, you will see a cross silhouetted against the skyline, whilst in front of you, a gully comes down from the left, carrying a small watercourse. At this point you should turn left from the track and ascend the hillside above the gully. By doing this you will locate the large water-filled mine workings called Crazywell, Classonwell or Classiwell Pool.

The legend attached to this pool is that either a wailing voice calls the name of the next person to die in the parish of Walkhampton or, on Midsummer's Eve, a reflection of the next victim can be seen. The pool is also said to be bottomless – the combined lengths of the bell ropes of Walkhampton Church tied together would not reach the bottom (which would make it more than 500 feet deep). However, the general depth of the pool is probably about

15 feet, but it is possible that there is a shaft in the middle, helping to perpetuate this legend. It is an old tin working and there is a great deal of evidence of this ancient Dartmoor industry. Another story says that the Well or Pool rises and falls with the tide at Plymouth, as it is connected by a massive underground tunnel. Such tales as these probably evolved in order to deter people from going there, resulting in the place name of Classiewell (1638) turning into the Crazywell Pool of today. Whatever the state of the tide, it is better not to get too near!

If the weather is clear, you will see the tip of the mast at North Hessary Tor, the top of which is the highest (man-made) point in the south of England. If you head towards it, you will strike the Devonport Leat, rattling along towards Raddick Hill. Follow the leat in the direction it flows for the next mile or so; you will be rewarded with fairly easy terrain and spectacular views.

Burrator is ringed with a number of impressive tors: Leather Tor, Sheeps Tor and Down Tor are the principal peaks.

From the lofty heights of the Devonport Leat, these can all be seen, the first two rising in stony grandeur, like great rocky cathedrals, from the forest surrounding Burrator Lake.

The Devonport Leat wends its way around Raddick Hill before hurtling steeply and noisily downhill. You have to do the same, so take care as you descend the hillside. The Princetown side of the leat is slightly easier to navigate as the Burrator side has a few swampy areas. The fleet-footed leat-follower should not find it too difficult to descend to the iron launder, which carries the leat over the River Meavy.

Once across the aqueduct, the second half of the walk becomes easier. The ground conditions beside the leat afford easy progress, and the lovely surroundings can be appreciated without too much distraction. Perhaps by now you may be a bit inquisitive about this wondrous, winding watercourse that you are following.

It is many miles long and is fed by the Blackbrook, Cowsic and West Dart rivers.

Crazywell Pool © Christian Hacker

It was opened in 1793, and largely satisfied the needs of Plymouth and Devonport until 1898 when Burrator Reservoir was opened. The Devonport Leat superseded the 17-mile long Drake's Leat, which often dried up in summer and froze in winter.

The leat enters Stanlake Plantation and the first of two stiles along this section has to be negotiated. Trout are known to be visible in the leat and, on a good day, walking at a gentle pace, it may be possible to see more than a hundred.

Unlike many woodland walks, in predominantly coniferous surroundings, this section has enough twists and turns, open glades and variety of flora, to create

an extremely interesting time. In the clearing below the impressive Leather Tor, there are fine views across to Sheeps Tor and down the reservoir towards Meavy.

Stay with the leat along its banks, ignoring all other paths and distractions, until you reach the first cross, which appears to have been slightly guillotined. This point is known as Cross Gate and the road which leads downhill serves as the way back to the starting point. In a short while a broader road, which circumnavigates the reservoir, will be reached and not long after this your vehicle will be seen. This is a peaceful walk and it is not unusual to be the only walker at any time of year.

WALK 4

CADOVER BRIDGE & DARTMOOR-ON-SEA

Cadover Bridge could be called Dartmoor-on-Sea because, on fine days, many hundreds of people, mainly Plymothians, congregate here en masse to enjoy this popular beauty spot. Situated on the River Plym, it is a jewel set in a landscape pitted with enormous china clay quarries – a vitally important raw material for so many industries. Its location on the south-western corner of Dartmoor, not too many miles from Plymouth, is the key to its popularity and it is well signposted from most directions. However, before you declare that you want to walk on Dartmoor to get away from the masses, not to join them, be assured that on leaving the car park you will soon be able to enjoy, in virtual solitude, a lovely, almost spectacular, four-mile walk of both woodland and open moor.

— DISTANCE: 4 miles
Ⓟ PARKING: Cadover Bridge car park
PL7 5EH

Park in the large car park (PL7 5EH) on the south bank of the Plym, just below the bridge before heading south-westwards, away from the bridge, over the stile and with Cadover behind you. The first part of the walk is generally easy: for the main part it follows the Pipe Track. This is aptly named as it follows the line of a pipe that carried china clay in suspension (water) down to the drying kilns at Shaugh Bridge, where you will be later.

The path is pleasant, and how much water you see or hear in the Plym, deep in the valley below, will depend on the season. North Wood can seem almost jungle-like in high summer but very stark in the depths of winter. In between times are probably the best, when spring is in the air or autumn covers this valley with a golden cloak.

North Wood is soon left behind as the track contours the side of West Down. On the opposite side of the valley, the great crags of the Dewerstone can be seen where climbers often test their skills; if your eyesight is good you may well see tiny figures dangling across these rocks. Later you will get to the top of the rocks – by the relatively easy route.

It is now time to apply the brakes as, after several hundred yards of gentle downward movement, the track begins to descend far more steeply, with the full force of gravity coming into play. Shaugh Bridge is a beauty spot and it is also an alternative starting/finishing place for this walk. The geographical term for a meeting place of

Cadover Bridge

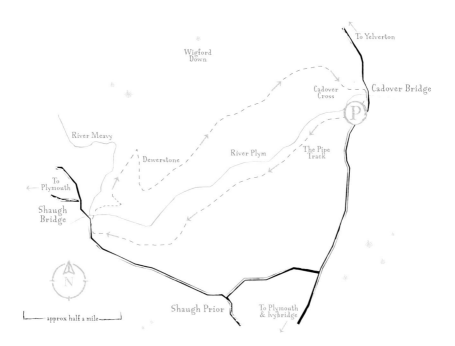

two rivers is a confluence. Here the Plym is joined by its major tributary, the Meavy. Older locals, and Dartmoor specialists, refer to it as the Mewy, a name which has origins in 'mew', meaning a seagull.

You are at the lowest point of the walk here. In times of heavy rain on the high moors these two watercourses can become raging torrents. The Meavy is less of a threat as its waters are controlled in part by Burrator Reservoir (opened in 1898 to supply Plymouth), many miles upstream. The Plym has removed various bridges in times of anger but, hopefully, the latest footbridge spanning the Plym will be intact. You only have to cross one river in order to reach the spur between the Plym and the Meavy, so do not cross Shaugh Bridge!

Your time with these two rivers is brief for the path you follow is along neither. Instead, you take the rough and rocky way, in the first instance, to a sharp bend to the left. Your possible breathlessness will be greatly relieved as the track levels out to pass a disused quarry before heading on to the right. The track was once a horse-drawn railway and the observant wayfarer will detect evidence of this inclined plane, if one is so inclined! Whether you have an interest in industrial archaeology or not, this is the path to follow upwards for the next half mile. After a long, semi-straight upward section, the track doubles back on itself and, as you approach the summit, becomes far more regular.

Dewerstone

As promised earlier, now is your chance to visit the rocks on the edge of the Dewerstone, partly for a well-earned rest, and partly to look at the view from this high rocky pinnacle. The rest of the walk is comparatively easy. Wigford Down is gentle and you skirt the edge of it, heading back towards Cadover Bridge along and above the field enclosures on the right. Leaving the former Ironage hill fort on top of the Dewerstone, you have an easy walk of just over three-quarters of a mile to the next point of interest, which is the large stone cross near Cadover Bridge. The head of the cross is original, but the lower part of its shaft is a replacement; soldiers out on manoeuvres in 1873 found and set up the head of the cross. In 1901 a cow knocked it down, so the new shaft was put in.

From the cross you should be able to see your vehicle in the car park on the opposite bank and by crossing Cadover Bridge, you will soon reach it.

Shaugh Bridge © Mike Frost

Sharp Tor

WALK 5

HARFORD & DARTMOOR LANDSCAPE

Harford is a hamlet along a picturesque country lane (with a generous number of passing places) which wends its way high on the hillside above the Erme Valley from Ivybridge. According to signposts, it is only about two and a half miles from Ivybridge to Harford, but it will inevitably seem further due to the twisting nature of this road.

— DISTANCE: 3 miles
℗ PARKING: Cadover PL21 0JQ

On reaching Harford Church, turn right onto the 'no through road'. This will take you uphill to some gates (which, hopefully, a willing volunteer will leap out of the car to open) at the entrance to a car park, which can accommodate about thirty or forty vehicles.

This is a three-mile walk, which is best done on a relatively clear day, mainly so as to enjoy the extensive views, but also to allow you to follow the route instructions more easily. If you have a compass/smartphone map, it would be useful as this part of the moor is prone to swift weather changes. The scenery around here is quite beautiful; a true Dartmoor landscape, even though it lacks the usual abundance of tors.

From the car park you will need to follow the wall, which you will keep on your left as you head in a general northward direction. When, after a few hundred yards, it starts to bend away from you to head downhill,

stop following it. Instead you will need to practice the art of 'contouring'. This means that instead of going up or down, you remain on the same level; the only drawback to contouring is having to walk as if one leg is longer than the other! Fortunately, this side of the Erme Valley is not too precipitous, and you can proceed ahead for several hundred yards over reasonable ground, even when there is no track to follow. Soon you will see another wall, also contouring along the hillside. Follow it, on the moor side, and it will carry you to Piles Gate, from where you will begin the steepest climb on the walk – up to Sharp Tor.

Sharp Tor is a bit of a misnomer, as it is not a sharp landscape feature nor are its rocks jagged. In fact, they are ideal for resting on to survey the views it offers over central southern Dartmoor and of south-west Devon. Away to the west you will see the china clay spoil heaps of Lee Moor; the sprawling urban mass of Plymouth and its Sound are also clearly discernible. You may well appreciate a breather here as it has been a bit of a climb, but the rest of the walk is a doddle.

River Erme, Ivy Bridge © Jamie Quinn

The River Erme, which flows hundreds of feet below, is regarded as one of the most beautiful in Devon. From here it flows in a generally southward direction for about another twelve miles before reaching the sea at Mothecombe.

Just a little to the north-west, deep down in the valley, is Piles Copse, a wood of stunted pendunculated oak trees, one of three such woods on the moor, (the other two are Black Tor Copse, above Meldon Reservoir on the West Okement River, and Wistman's Wood, about three-quarters of a mile above Two Bridges on the West Dart River). Wistman's Wood is a particularly fine example of how such trees survive in the face of adversity – Dartmoor can be a wild, wet and windy place, so if you have chosen one of its more benign days for this stroll, you should congratulate yourself! An average of 180 rain days a year, combined

with a low temperature, produces a soil that only the most stubborn and resistant of trees can handle.

At the time when the climate was marginally warmer and less wet, this part of Dartmoor was particularly favoured by Bronze Age people; there are many pounds, stone rows, stone circles and other remains here as evidence of their previous existence. However, it is a more recent piece of history which will help you on your way. Just a few hundred yards to the east you will see a track, again running along the hillside. Go across to it and then follow it southwards. This is the track bed of the Redlake Mineral Railway, which was opened in 1911. It covered seven and a half miles, from the southern tip of the moor at Western Beacon, up to Redlake. About a hundred workers produced the clay that was carried down this line, a venture which finished, forever, in 1932. The lines had all disappeared by the end of the following year.

When you reach the track bed you will also see a row of boundary stones running alongside the line. Follow the railway for about 300 yards. At the end of the straight, you should see a slightly elevated slope on your right. This is Piles Hill and to ensure you are on the right route, you should be able to see the Longstone, just a short distance away from the cairn, to the south-east.

In order to get back to your vehicle at Harford Moor Gate, it will now be necessary to test either your sense of direction, or your map skills.

The most direct line is not all that apparent as you stand on this gently rounded hill of three sides. To get your bearings, look to the south-west where you will see a small clump of trees on a level down. The down is called Hanger Down so, not surprisingly, the clump is called Hanger Down Clump (it is about two miles away). If you make a beeline for this, you will descend the hill over uneven ground.

After a short distance on the descent you will see, just on the other side of the valley, Tristis Rock (also called Hall Tor), which you should keep well to your right. All being well, you should soon complete this relatively easy, but immensely enjoyable, little walk.

Black Tor Casacde © Mike Frost

Wistman's Wood

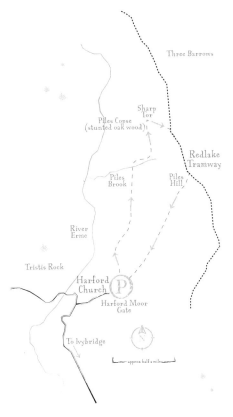

Three Barrows

Sharp Tor

Piles Copse
(stunted oak wood)

Redlake Tramway

Piles Brook

Piles Hill

River Erme

Tristis Rock

Harford Church

Harford Moor Gate

To Ivybridge

approx half a mile

WALK 6

SHIPLEY BRIDGE & THE AVON DAM

Shipley Bridge is one of the loveliest locations in Devon as it lies on the River Avon, about two miles to the north-north-west of South Brent. Although it can be approached from South Brent, the lane is tortuous, and those unfamiliar with the twists and turns of the road may prefer to reach the destination by the signposted road which leads from the Marley Head junction on the A38. This climbs over the shoulder of the distinctive Brent Hill and is a slightly less nerve-wracking way to get to Shipley Bridge (Avon Dam). Dartmoor National Park has a car park in the area although some choose to park along the road by the bridge.

> — DISTANCE: 5 miles (3 miles if reduced)
> Ⓟ PARKING: Shipley Bridge TQ10 9ED

The first section of this walk is ideal for those accompanied by youngsters in prams, or people in wheelchairs. A well-surfaced road leads up the valley from Shipley Bridge to the Avon Dam. The route includes the dam and a section on the moor walking around 5 miles; however, the walk can be shortened to 3 miles by walking up to the dam and returning along the same route.

It has a gentle gradient of about one and a half miles up to the dam where the remains of buildings, which form the western margin of the car park, are the former clay dries where clays were processed after being brought down the few miles from Bala Brook Head. In a short distance you will see a largish rock beside the road on the left-hand side. This is the Hunters' Stone. On

it you may be able to identify the names of once celebrated local huntsmen who rode these moors in the past. To the right of the path, the River Avon can be seen tumbling steeply downwards in a perpetual rush to reach the sea at Bigbury Bay. Its local name is the Aune, and the map proudly proclaims the point where it rises as Aune Head – a remote, wild and wet location.

A gateway with stone pillars is soon reached but more noticeable is the jungle of rhododendrons that line this next section of the walk. The gateway was the entrance to Brentmoor House, once a substantial moorland residence; for several years, prior to its demolition in 1968, it was a youth hostel. In its grounds, close to the side of the hill and amidst the rhododendrons, you may care to leave the track to seek out the memorial to a little girl who died here.

Above this former house the road crosses the Avon and follows the east bank

River Avon © Peter Morrison

Brentor Church

Rhododendrons

valley. However, if it's a northerly breeze or even a north-easterly, you have to walk hard to make progress up the valley! The trough-like nature of this section of the valley has earned it the name 'Long-a-Traw'.

Ahead lies the Avon Dam, an impressive structure designed to store water for people in the Totnes and South Hams areas. On stormy days, there is usually shelter in the lee of the dam. If you find yourself speculating as to what it would be like should the dam suddenly burst, you can be reassured that this is a geologically stable region, and the dam has stood here, quite undisturbed, since the mid-1950s. In times of severe drought, when the level of the reservoir drops, an ancient settlement is revealed on the north-east side of the lake, close to where the Brockhill streams enters it.

northwards. Should there be a strong prevailing westerly wind blowing, you will appreciate the sheltered nature of this

Now is the time to turn around and retrace your steps if you wish to undertake the shorter walk. However, if you would like to continue you may wish to pick up the Abbots' Way, a well-defined track on the north-east side of the reservoir. This ancient routeway linked abbeys on opposing sides of Dartmoor.

Walk for around 500 yards above the top of the lake, and you will reach a crossing point over the Avon, close to where the Western Wella Brook arrives from the north. The way back to the dam lies along the steeper sloping western bank of the reservoir and the route back to Shipley is all downhill!

Shipley Tor

Avon Dam

Dartmoor pony

WALK 7

HOLNE MOOR & WHEAL EMMA

The beautiful moorland parish of Holne contains some of the finest scenery in Devon. This walk includes a mixture of open moorland punctuated by deep wooded combes, some filled with quiet babbling brooks, others with strong torrents. It is a dramatic and yet relatively unknown walk.

— DISTANCE: 3 miles
Ⓟ PARKING: Western Beacon Quarry

The starting point for this lovely little walk is a car park in Western Beacon Quarry, now disused. Situated about half a mile to the north-west of Holne, it is easiest to reach from the A38 at Ashburton. Follow the signs for the River Dart Country Park as far as the entrance to the park, then continue along this meandering road, which leads over the lovely Holne Bridge. Beyond it is a steep hill, where it's necessary to bear left and follow the signs towards Holne village.

As you approach Holne, you will find that the road towards the moor doesn't actually pass through the village centre but veers to its right and starts to climb towards the open moor. The walk's starting point is immediately on your left-hand side, just beyond the cattle grid. There is enough room for about eight to ten cars. If you arrive from the Hexworthy direction, the disused quarry will be on your right, immediately above the cattle grid.

Come out of the car park entrance and turn right onto the track which leads towards 'Stone Shallows', also known as 'The Shanty'. Do not enter this private property but, on reaching it, head right and follow its edge for a short distance. At the end of the wall, the track climbs slightly more steeply. The track has a kink and in about 20 yards you should fork off to the right.

A small stream is soon encountered but is easily negotiated. You are heading for the top of the highest enclosed field that you can see ahead of you. Don't worry – the terrain is easy on the foot and the track climbs gently all the way up.

On reaching the top of this field the route becomes more of a path, and you should follow it along the stone wall. If you have not yet stopped to enjoy the view, then now is a good time! You are on the high edge of the open rolling southern moor. To the south-east the land falls away dramatically to create a tremendous view of a large part of eastern Dartmoor and a vast area of South Devon. From some angles

Holne Bridge

Dartmoor Landscape, looking towards Dart Valley

you will be able to see Buckfast Abbey through a gap in the nearby hills. Beyond lies the beautiful countryside that fringes the great tourist area of Torbay. As the wall on the left ends, you will see a dry watercourse contouring the hill lower down the hillside; this is the Wheal Emma. It is one of many on Dartmoor which once provided a source of power for machinery. 'Wheal' is an old Celtic word for mine, and wheals are found through Devon and Cornwall.

Avoid the temptation to go straight down the hill. It is easier to contour the hillside for a short time before gradually dropping down to the leat. The Wheal Emma Leat was cut in 1859; it ran all the way from the Swincombe River, a tributary of the West Dart, and around the hills for nine miles, bringing extra water to the River Mardle. The latter was the source of waterpower for a number of mining operations including the Wheal Emma copper mine (hence the leat's name) near Buckfastleigh. This mine joined forces with the nearby Brockwood Mine to form a company called South Devon United. The golden age for this undertaking was between 1861 and 1877, when many thousands of tons of copper were raised. The workings, in the valleys below, went more than 700 feet below ground.

Two small footbridges cross it but today they remain redundant. If you walk along the bed of the former leat, take care to look up occasionally as a small tree grows in the centre of it at one point.

You are not going to follow the leat too far but stay with it until you reach a point where a track comes down the hill to cross it, and six slabs of granite form a bridge

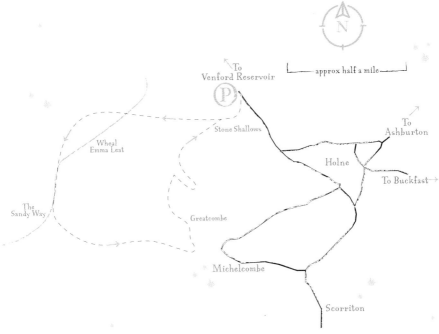

over it. There are other tracks and further bridges, but this is the one you require. Turn left and go downhill along the path, known as the Sandy Way. Follow this route and the signpost for Michelcombe.

The Sandy Way is an ancient path which, in early times, was probably used as a major trackway between Ashburton and Tavistock. The lane, most likely an old cattle droving route, descends for about half a mile to reach the hamlet of Michelcombe. Although it is a stony thoroughfare, it remains a pleasant corridor as it passes between fields – often containing sheep.

Almost at the bottom of this hill, a signposted track off to the left should be taken. This immediately passes an attractive cottage before crossing a stream supplemented by water from the Holne Moor Leat. Alas, what has gone down must now go up! This track must be followed in order to regain the dizzy heights of Holne Moor. Although the way is steep, the many twists and turns in the track and the path make it an enjoyable climb.

At the end of the path there are no indicators to point the way. If you ascend the hill you will see the extensive rooftops of 'The Shanty' to your right. If you keep this to your right and head back over the moor, you should have no difficulty in relocating the quarry. The view now lies across the Double Dart, over Holne Chase and beyond to Buckland Beacon.

Buckland Beacon

WALK 8

HAYTOR & THE BEST TORS ON DARTMOOR

Haytor, on eastern Dartmoor, is one of the best-known landmarks in Devon. Every year several thousand visitors park their cars beneath the rock and stroll up to its twin granite masses. Over one third of the Devonshire landscape can be seen from this vantage point. Many people settle for this brief excursion as their day out on Dartmoor; they return home unaware of the delights and attractions in the vicinity of this famous old rock. Here is a walk in an area of unparalleled beauty, steeped in history and legend.

— DISTANCE: 6 miles
Ⓟ PARKING: Haytor TQ13 9XT

The lower car park at Haytor provides free parking. The first stage of the walk is not up to the tor but north-westwards to the disused quarries on the north-east shoulder of Haytor. Should it be a windy day when you explore this area, you will find this large quarry a pleasant haven as it is well-sheltered from the elements. On a sunny day it can be a suntrap, and at such times walkers may be reluctant to leave, especially if there is a biting wind. In the quarry is a pond, which is far deeper than it appears, and care should be taken when nearby.

Leading from the quarry is the first railroad to have been built in Devon. However, its main claim to fame is that the lines were made of granite from the quarries, this being cheaper and more accessible than imported metal for the rails. The granite-quarrying enterprise, which began in 1820 with great optimism, faltered less than half a century later, in the face of competition from more easily accessible Cornish granites. Your route lies, for about one hundred yards, along the branch line leading out of the Haytor quarry to a junction with the main tramway line. Before you head north-eastwards across Haytor Down towards Black Hill, it may be worth examining the 'points', also of granite, which switched the wagons toward their destination.

The beauty of the stroll to Black Hill is that the terrain is so gentle on the feet that the rambler can enjoy the surroundings at every step. At this point you can choose to take in the view of distant tankers in the English Channel, or maybe scan the far horizons of Somerset's hills. However, at the cairn on Black Hill there is only one way to look, and that is down into the valleys of the Becka Brook and Bovey rivers.

Haytor

Some skills are now necessary to reach the desired path. The way down from Black Hill is steep and the force of gravity will be all too apparent: it will be necessary to apply the brakes on this next section. A generally northward direction needs to be followed, for a few hundred yards, until a rough track running above the fields is met. On reaching it, follow it left, or westwards. After a short stretch of gentle gradients, it plunges down the hillside towards the steep depression carved by the Becka Brook. The large hill immediately ahead of you is Manaton Rocks, which is featured in another of the walks in this book.

By now you will have seen some of the different types of scenery on Eastern Dartmoor. It is an area well-served by a complicated network of country lanes and it is almost impossible to get lost around here! With such 'famous last words' ringing in your ears, skirt the edge of Leighon to stay with the path that runs around the hillside on a southward course. Beyond two fields, which will be on your left-hand side, the track will drop down on its way to cross the Becky Brook. If you are going to encounter muddy conditions on this walk, then this next section is the most likely spot. Following this, there is a sharp climb

Hound Tor

Leighon

cairn on
Blackhill

Hound
Tor

Medieval
Village

Greator Rocks

Chinkwell Tor

Bell Tor

Haytor Granite
Tramway

Holwell Tor

Haytor
Quarry

Becky Brook

To Bovey
Tracey

Bonehill
Rocks

Haytor
Rocks

P

To
Widecombe

Saddle Tor

Top Tor

Emsworthy
Mire

Hemsworthy
Gate

Rippon Tor

To
Ashburton

approx half a mile

upwards on the other side of the valley but, if you keep in mind that there is some great moor and tor landscape ahead, it is worth the climb.

One natural attraction and one man-made are the rewards on reaching the open moor once more. The tor on your left is called Greator Rocks and has several summits which are ideal for clambering over, or simply to sit on, in order to survey the surrounding scenery. Ahead lies the Hound Tor mediaeval village, which was excavated in 1961. This settlement was probably abandoned in the fourteenth century, possibly because of the devastating effects of the Black Death, a plague which killed almost half the population of north-west Europe. This farming community had about a dozen buildings. Corn was grown in the small fields and animals were grazed on the poorer pastures. It must have been a remote existence, but several generations of families lived there, from the tenth century up to the death of the village four centuries later.

Hound Tor, the next destination, is one of the largest rock piles on Dartmoor and its closeness to a road assures it of

Saddle Tor

Bonehill Rocks © www.flickr.com/photos/chris-parker

public attention; on fine days many people will be found scrambling over the various piles. There are apparent gaps between the various columns of rock, which makes Hound Tor a fine example of an 'avenue tor'.

Sometimes it is difficult to give precise directions in a book such as this and, when people misinterpret well-intentioned route directions, it can invariably lead to them getting lost. Some are philosophical in such a situation, whereas others write to the author! The next bit needs to be followed carefully and it calls for a sense of awareness.

Most walkers have an aversion to road walking, so to minimise the pounding on tarmac for this outing, it is necessary to head almost south, or slightly west of it, across Houndtor Down. If you are not carrying a compass, you can work out your course by observing a row of trees that line the road, which leads southwards also. By steering a walking course parallel to them, until the last is reached, and then heading to where a dry stone wall comes down to meet this road, you will cut down the road walking section to just a few hundred yards. Walk along the right side of the road, downhill, and you will learn from a sign on the opposite side that bulls in fields with heifers or cows are not likely to cause walkers any problems. Feeling much enlightened from this gem of country lore, cross the cattle grid, where you will regain open moorland.

Turn right and strike out away from the road. You will see, almost immediately, the rockpile of Bell Tor on your right. However, this is not your destination and you should head to the left of this as it has the advantage of enabling you to skirt some boggy terrain.

The next landmark is one of the most pleasing-to-the-eye rock piles of the 234 (or so) tors on the moor. Bonehill Rocks gives an excellent view down the valley of the East Webburn, with the tall church tower of St Pancras of Widecombe-in-the-Moor a readily identifiable landmark. Top Tor lies just over half a mile to the south-south-east of Bonehill Rocks and is the next point to head for. Although there is a general upward trend in the walking required to reach this tor, the gradient is mild and the going underfoot is very accommodating. Walking on moorland like this is far less demanding on calf muscles than on stony tracks or surfaced roads.

Top Tor is appropriately named and gives a greater panoramic view than many of the tors visited in this walk. If the weather is clear enough you will be able to see, about 10 miles away to the west, North Hessary Tor transmitting station, above Princetown.

For the next mile or so the main Widecombe to Haytor road will be in view, so the name of the game will be to avoid having to walk on its hard surface, or to dodge its traffic. This is no problem.

When you've finished enjoying the view from Top Tor, head down towards Hemsworthy Gate, a junction where the road from Ashburton meets the Widecombe road. Keep an eye open for the ghost of a horseman, who is supposed to rides the road from Haytor towards Hemsworthy. Don't bear too far to the right on a line from Top Tor to Hemsworthy Gate, as this is an area of very wet land a and it would be such a shame to be dry on

Chinkwell Tor

reaching the final section of the walk, only to become engulfed in a foul-smelling mire! However, although it's prone to wetness, it's not a dangerously boggy patch.

From Hemsworthy Gate you will need to stay quite close to, but not necessarily on, the road for a very short while. On your left is Saddle Tor. Once you have climbed over this rocky hill, you will see Haytor Rocks. Saddle Tor is so named because, when seen from a distance, in tandem with Haytor, the elevated feature resembles a saddle. It is more than likely that you will have climbed sufficient rocks today as is necessary to satiate your climbing requirements. Haytor, like the others, is optional. It is quite easy to pass by the base of this eminent pile, and enjoy its wondrous view over South Devon, before heading downhill to your vehicle in the lower car park.

The map says you have done about six miles but, if you have indulged in the energetic pursuits of tor climbing, your body will no doubt tell you that you have done more!

Benett's Cross © Alex Graeme

WALK 9

YELVERTON - WARREN HOUSE &
THE LAND OF MINES

This expedition takes us to an area of former tin mines, with such great names as Vitifer and the Golden Dagger Mine. There are two possible starting points; you can park near the famous Warren House Inn, on the B3212, a few miles to the north-east of Postbridge or you can park in the small car park at Bennett's Cross, less than half a mile along the same road towards Moretonhampstead. Bennett's Cross is a rough-hewn piece of granite with a minimum amount of masonry effort spent upon it. The 'WB' initials are believed to stand for Warren Bounds. A warren is a place where rabbits were kept for breeding, and later eating; they were the basic diet for the tinners who toiled away in the bowels of the earth all around the district. Their pub was on the opposite side of the road to the inn you see today; its name is another acknowledgement of the importance of rabbits.

— DISTANCE: 4 miles
ⓟ PARKING: Warren House Inn PL20 6TA
or Bennetts Cross PL20 6TA

If you parked near the Warren House, where there is a small car park on the left (just before the inn if you are travelling towards Postbridge) you will find a broad track heading straight out of it. For its first few hundred yards you will walk parallel with a line of telegraph poles, which will not be too far away at any time in the first mile or so of the walk. To reach the valley bottom by the most direct route, leave the main track, not far from the lower slopes of the hill, to descend a much steeper and rougher track. This takes you to a point where you can easily cross the small Redwater Brook,

which runs down from Bennett's Cross. If you start from Bennett's Cross, you need to make your way southwards for a short distance until you pick up the depression of the Redwater Brook, which will take you down to the same point. Almost until the very end of the walk, the route will be identical.

The tin mines, which later also produced iron ore, operated from the early eighteenth century through to about the time of the First World War. As you head eastwards towards Headland Warren, you will see the enormous gulleys associated with the industry. Long gone are the waterwheels that operated the crushing stamps, as are the miners' cottages and the ponies which carted away the products of their efforts.

The tin miners were a hardy breed of men and a pub filled with them, after they had done a hard day's work, was not a place for the mild-mannered or faint-hearted!

The tracks in this vicinity will spare you the problem of negotiating the gulleys, which you would find, should you ever traverse them, a very time-consuming, energy-draining version of a moorland big-dipper.

From the valley bottom you will see a path climbing the hillside, to the right of the poles and to the left of a stone-walled enclosure. The hill starts gently but becomes a bit steeper. The path takes us high to a col, or pass, between Challacombe and Birch Tor. It will not be long before you reach Headland Warren Farm. Long ago, this was the Birch Tor Inn, another meeting place for tin miners. It bore a sign on its door which informed any uninitiated customers that "Jan Roberts lives here and sells whisky and beer, your hearts for to cheer; and if you want meat, to make up a treat, here be rabbits to eat." James Hannaford lived here with his dog in the last part of the nineteenth century. He would walk more or less the same route that you have covered so far on this trek. Unfortunately, on one occasion, he got too near one of the old shafts and toppled in, only being saved from certain death by some handily-placed timbers. His dog sat at the top of the shaft until a search party arrived in the vicinity, when he barked for all he was worth, leading them to rescue a badly injured, but very grateful, man.

As you descend to this settlement, turn right onto a signed bridlepath beside this dwelling. Walk past the stable block and along the surfaced road for the shortest of distances. On your right is a gate with 'footpath' clearly marked on it. Now we leave Headland Warren and its colourful past behind. There is a most pleasant and level path leading up in a southerly direction. It is quite probable that this section will be the most sheltered along the route, as the prevailing wind is a westerly flow and you have the great hill of Challacombe Down to protect you.

Leave the confines of Headland Warren via a gate in a stone wall. The going underfoot is excellent, apart from a narrow piece of boggy ground, which needs to be side-stepped. By more or less staying on the same level, you will soon reach a short terrace of three cottages – Challacombe Cottages – and farther on another dwelling and outbuildings. Head on past them, but steer right and climb up to a gateway with a signpost. Head in the direction of Bennett's Cross and in the next few hundred yards you will change direction from south, through west, to north. At the same time, it's likely your leeward aspect will be replaced by a windward one and progress may be impeded if the westerly wind is wild this day.

A moorland view thus gives way to a forest view as the enormous plantation of Soussons Down will be seen away to the left. Just over half a mile away to the south west and on the southern edge of the forest, is a little hill which has the strange name of Ephraim's Pinch, where legend has it that poor Ephraim met an untimely death trying to prove his worthiness to his would-be father-in-law. The path though is still easy and drops down to an old-fashioned form of stile. There is a clump of trees on the right side of your desired track and a forest beyond the stream. In between

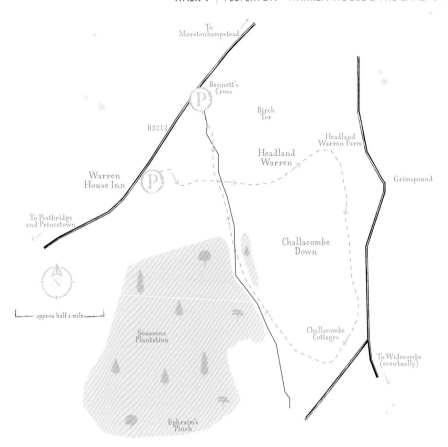

are many more industrial remains from the mining days of this valley. There are buildings, and a curious circular structure known as a buddle (a shallow inclined container in which tin ore was washed), plus a disued dry leat lying below the track. Follow this route until you cross the tiny trickle of a stream where you should ignore the left-hand signposted track.

Instead, proceed on up the west bank of the stream and you will reach the point where you were at the start. Those bound for Bennett's Cross will carry on straight ahead. Anyone heading back to the Warren House and, no doubt a well-earned drink, will need to bear left and climb the hill, once

more beside the poles, in a west-bound direction, to reach their vehicle.

This is a stroll of about four miles and the bulk of it has been relatively easy, apart the bits which weren't!

Bennett's Cross

WALK 10

MANATON & MANATON ROCKS

Manaton is a small village about five miles north-west of Bovey Tracey. James Galsworthy lived here for many years and wrote The Forsyte Saga, amongst other works, which is only a few hundred yards from the start of this walk. At just under three miles, the walk begins from the car park near the church. It is just one of many which could be done in this part of Dartmoor as it is particularly well blessed with many miles of signposted footpaths.

—— DISTANCE: 3 miles
Ⓟ PARKING: Manaton TQ13 9UJ

Enter the churchyard through the Lych Gate (Lych derives from a German word 'leich' meaning corpse, so it was where the coffin was rested before Christian burial). Pass in front of the church and, in the shortest of distances, you will be confronted with an immediate choice of routes. Turn right and follow the path which includes a stile. This path leads up to Manaton Rocks – an easy pile to clamber over – and an extensive view to the north; not the typical view of rolling open moorland, more a cultivated landscape of fields and woods.

Beyond Manaton Rocks, the path descends the hill quite sharply and in a short distance it is necessary to bear right on to a much more level path, which leads to a surfaced road. On this section, make sure that you watch out for any embedded stones that

protrude a few critical inches above the ground.

On meeting the road, turn right onto it and climb up and over the brow of the hill. In a short distance, take the first turn on the left, which is a surfaced road passing some attractive houses. This ends with a cattle grid. Ignore the obvious surfaced track ahead and bear left, heading diagonally downwards across the field to the bottom corner. Go through the gateway, across a small field, through another gateway, and then a few yards straight ahead you should see a stone wall. Look for a further gateway on your right which will take you into the Neadon Cleave East Dartmoor Nature Reserve. Turn left at the signpost and follow the footpath through the woods, dropping downhill – first gently and then more steeply.

A road is met at what appears to be the bottom of the hill. Turn right and walk along it towards Foxworthy Bridge. After a few

Bowerman's Nose, close to Manaton

Foxworthy
Bridge

Bovey
Woodlands

Manaton
Rocks

Horsham

River
Bovey

Manaton

B3344

Kes Tor
Inn

N

To Becky Falls &
Bovey Tracey

approx half a mile

hundred yards this road bends and drops more steeply towards the River Bovey. Before you reach the river there is a path signposted for Neadon Cleave, off to your right, which should be followed. Apart from the occasional muddy patch, this is an easy path contouring the valley side of Neaden Cleave. Along this section you may like to play 'Spot the Nesting Boxes'. It will depend upon the season as to whether or not these detached residences for our feathered friends are occupied.

Eventually you'll meet a T-junction with a path coming straight down the hill. If you have some surplus energy, you can go downhill, turning left at the bottom and within yards you will reach Horsham Steps, a miniature version of Becky Falls: a lovely spot for a picnic or rest. If, however, you wish to get back to the car more quickly, you must turn right at the T-junction and climb steeply upwards. Whatever your choice, you will have to climb this steep

Bovey Woods © Christian Hacker

slope sooner or later. It is the hardest climb on the walk, and it is always worth pausing to 'enjoy the view' – even if it is obscured by trees!

Continue with the path, ignoring the one coming down from the right, and on reaching some lovely old cottages, turn right and head for 'Manaton', not 'Water'. The track is a good one and it should not be too long before you see Manaton Church on the left and ahead of you as you walk through the gate.

Refreshments are available at the Kestor Inn and Becky Falls (seasonal and subject to opening times), another half mile further on. When rested, you will have completed three miles – definitely worth an ice cream!

Jay, taken on Dartmoor

Becky Falls

The Downs © Gilly Dowdell